HOW TO PLAY
JAZZ
PIANO

Pam Wedgwood

For online audio tracks
scan the QR code or go to
fabermusic.com/content/audio

FABER _ff_ MUSIC

Contents

© 2018 by Faber Music Ltd
This edition first published in 2018
Bloomsbury House, 74–77 Great Russell Street, London WC1B 3DA
Music processed by Donald Thomson
Text designed by Susan Clarke
Cover design by adamhaystudio.com
Audio recorded and produced by Ned Bennett
Printed in England by Caligraving Ltd
All rights reserved

ISBN10: 0-571-53949-1
EAN13: 978-0-571-53949-9
To buy Faber Music publications or to find out about the full range of titles available
please contact your local music retailer or Faber Music sales enquiries:
Faber Music Ltd, Burnt Mill, Elizabeth Way, Harlow CM20 2HX
Tel: +44 (0) 1279 82 89 82   Fax: +44 (0) 1279 82 89 83
sales@fabermusic.com   fabermusicstore.com

Introduction

> Jazz is like a language. You learn the alphabet, which is the scales. You learn the sentences, which are the chords. And then you talk with your instrument …
> Stan Getz

Would you like to discover a whole new and exciting world of musical expression – but your heart sinks when you see a page full of complicated shapes and symbols? In this book I have tried to present all the fundamental elements you will need to play jazz piano in a fun and simple introduction that will work for everyone. We'll cover:

- understanding syncopated rhythms
- how to swing
- playing from memory
- understanding basic chords and chord symbols
- playing in different popular styles
- scales and modes used in jazz
- the beginnings of improvisation
- suggested listening to give you inspiration.

There are lots of audio tracks to listen to and play along with here: Where necessary, 2 bars of count-in beats are given.

I hope you will gain confidence from this book and want to go on to further study. To start with, all you need is a basic knowledge of how to play the piano, to approximately Grade 2 (Elementary-level) standard.

Don't be afraid to step out of your safety zone – just give it a try. Ready to get started? Let's go!

Session 1
Syncopation and ragtime

Syncopation is a rhythm which is played off the main beat(s) of the bar.

Style spotlight

The ragtime era began in the 1890s and made a feature of syncopated rhythm. Pieces were usually in $\frac{2}{4}$ or $\frac{4}{4}$, with a left-hand pattern of bass notes on strong beats (1 and 3) and chords on weak beats (2 and 4), accompanying a syncopated melody in the right hand. The name ragtime came from describing the syncopation as 'ragged' rhythm.

❶ Performance piece **Rocket rag!**

Listen to track 1 and clap the right-hand rhythm before playing this piece.

Style spotlight

A jazz waltz is in 3 time, in a jazzy style and usually features syncopation.
Here's an example: listen to it on track 2 first.

2 Performance piece **Raggy waltz**

Pam says

❝ Understanding syncopated rhythm will help you play jazz piano! ❞

Listening post: Ragtime

Easy Winners Scott Joplin
Maple Leaf Rag Scott Joplin
Joshua Rifkin has made a recording of Scott Joplin rags – they're really worth listening to
It's a Raggy Waltz Dave Brubeck – written in a more modern jazz style
Golliwog's Cakewalk Debussy
The Top Liner Rag Joseph Lamb
Charleston Rag/I'm Just Wild About Harry/Memories of You Eubie Blake

Scott Joplin (1868–1917) was the most famous ragtime composer. An African-American composer and pianist, Joplin became famous through the publication of his 'Maple Leaf Rag', which was hugely popular and brought him an income for life. 'The Entertainer' became well known when it was featured in the film 'The Sting' in 1972.

Pam says

❝ *The Entertainer* makes a great party piece – see if you can memorise it. Listening to the demo track will help. **❞**

③ Performance piece **The Entertainer**

Scott Joplin
arr. Pam Wedgwood

Session 2
Learning to swing

Style spotlight

Swing music became popular in America in the 1930–40s, and has had a huge influence on music ever since. One of the best-known swing musicians was Benny Goodman, who was known as the King of Swing.

The key feature of swing is its rhythm: ♪♪ is played slightly unevenly or 'swung'. The notes are written the same but are played differently:

♪♪ = ♩♪

♪♪ that are not swung are called 'straight'.

④ **Track 4** is played straight.

⑤ **Track 5** is played swung.

Listening post: Swing...

Ain't Misbehavin' Billie Holliday
Take the A Train Duke Ellington
Sentimental Journey Frank Sinatra
In the Mood Glen Miller
Mack the Knife Louise Armstrong
It's Only a Paper Moon Nat King Cole

⑥ **Baby bouncer**

Try playing this piece swung: listen to the demo track first.

Pam says

❝ Learning to play in swing rhythm is crucial to understanding how jazz rhythms work. Listen to as much swing music as you can – it will help you to feel the rhythm. ❞

7

Call and reponse

Pam says

" When jazz musicians get together they often use call-and-response to create music: one musician plays a phrase and a second player answers it. It's a musical question and answer! While this can form the whole tune, sometimes only a few lines in a verse are played this way. The idea originated in Africa and was brought to America by slaves. It influenced jazz, blues and rock music. **"**

Listen to each track all the way through before you see if you can copy each phrase – without looking at the music. Try this away from the piano first – clap or play with a wooden spoon on a saucepan for fun!

> **Listening post**
>
> **Dueling Banjos** Eric Weissberg and Steve Mandell
> **Say it Loud, I'm Black and I'm Proud** James Brown
> **Don't You just Know it** Huey 'Piano' Smith and The Clowns

12 Performance piece **Hot potato**

Session 3
Memory and ears

Jazz is an open-ended music designed for open minds.
Author unknown

It's well known that learning a musical instrument improves memory and intelligence. Research has shown that playing and listening stimulates your brain and expands your working memory capacity. For jazz musicians, memory and learning to listen are particularly important – memorising pieces and lyrics is an impressive achievement that improves performance and will help when learning to improvise.

To improve this skill, set yourself a daily task by selecting an easy piece and learning a few bars at a time from memory. Repetitions of these phrases will improve your memory skills. Learn to listen carefully to the music:
• Look out for patterns and the overall shape.
• Be aware of the key you're playing in and play the scale before you begin.
• Always use the same fingering.

Don't worry if it takes longer than you are expecting. It will come in the end. Gradually extend the number of bars you're learning until you know the whole piece. It's a great feeling when you achieve this and it will help your improvisation – and you'll be able to play spontaneously at parties without any music!

Pam says
❝ Improving your memory and listening skills will help you to recall little riffs and patterns when you're improvising. ❞

Memory workouts

Pam says

"Here are some short pieces to memorise. Listen to the track, then play each hand separately, then try hands together. Repeat each two- or four-bar phrase until you know it from memory."

13 Hot-dog blues

14 Performance piece Blues for baby

15 Swing into action

Learn this from memory then try it starting
on D or G. Memorising one or two bars at
a time is fine.

16 Swing-a-ling

Learn each phrase individually until you really know it,
then try playing it from memory.

⑰ Gee whizz!

Learn each phrase individually until you really know it. Then try playing it
from memory, then one note lower, starting on C (the key signature will be
F major, so remember the B flats).

⑱ Cheeky Charlie

Try this piece with both straight and swung. When you've memorised it, you
could try it in G major: starting on a G in the left hand, B in the right hand.
Remember to play F sharps!

19 Performance piece **Memory Lane**

Try to learn this longer piece from memory in four-bar phrases,
repeating them as often as needed. Listen to it lots first.

Session 4
The importance of intervals

Music is made up of different rhythms and pitches combined together. The pitches form different intervals (the distance between one note and another). If you give each note a number from 1 to 8, you can work out the size of the interval. Here are the intervals in a C major scale:

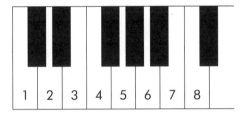

Pam says

" If you know what an interval sounds like and how to play it on the piano, it's much easier to make up your own tunes when you're improvising. "

Know your intervals

Here are some well-known tunes to help you recognise intervals. After you've played each, try singing the interval to develop your sense of pitch.

Interval of a 2nd: God save the Queen

Many other tunes feature this stepwise interval, but *Happy birthday to you!* and The Beatles' *Yesterday* are good examples to listen to.

Interval of a 3rd: The Blue Danube

Other good examples of this interval can be found in *Kumbaya* and *Michael, row the boat ashore*.

Interval of a 4th: Auld lang syne

You can also find this interval in *Amazing grace* and *O Christmas tree*.

Interval of a 5th: Twinkle twinkle little star

The theme from *Star Wars* and *Music of the night* (from *Phantom of the opera*) also feature fifths.

Interval of a 6th: My Bonnie lies over the ocean

The Entertainer features the interval of a sixth as well.

Intervals of a 7th and an octave

Can you find your own examples of 7ths and octaves and play them
by ear? Write them on the stave below if you like.

Try starting each tune on a different note. Use your ears (not the notation)
to work out how to play it correctly in the new key.

Spotting intervals in pieces

Listen to each piece before you play it, then circle the intervals indicated.
Don't forget the left hand!

20 Interval hunt!

Look for a 3rd, 4th, 5th and 7th in this piece. The first two have been
indicated.

21 Interval groovin'

Look for a 3rd, 4th, 5th and 7th in this piece.

㉒ Interval dreaming

Look for a 6th, 7th and an octave here.

Singing intervals

Play the first note then sing the second note before checking it on the keyboard.
Work it out by singing up from the key note. Finally, name the interval.

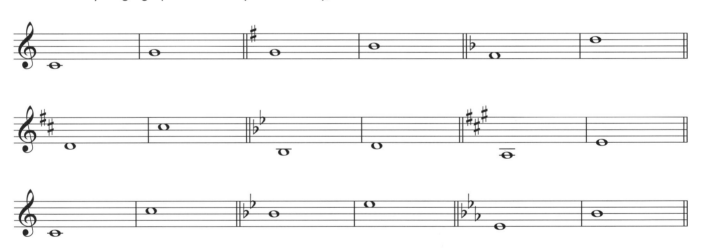

Code songs challenge

Intervals are worked out by counting up the notes of a scale. Try playing these
songs by following the number codes below – I've given you the key, opening
rhythm and starting note for each. Can you name the songs?

Song: _____

Key: C major (starting note C)

♩ ♩ ♩ ♩
1 1 5 5 6 6 5 4 4 3 3 2 2 1
5 5 4 4 3 3 2 5 5 4 4 3 3 2
1 1 5 5 6 6 5 4 4 3 3 2 2 1

Song: _____

Key: C major (starting note C)

♩. ♪ ♩ ♪
1 2 3 1 3 1 3 2 3 4 4 3 2 4
3 4 5 3 5 3 5 4 5 6 6 5 4 6
5 1 2 3 4 5 6 6 2 3 4 5 6 7 ...

Session 5
Starting to improvise

> **One of the things I like about jazz is that I don't know what's going to happen next.**
> Bix Beiderbecke

One of the note patterns that is most commonly used in music is the pentatonic scale – a group of 5 notes.

Pam says

" Studying the pentatonic scale will give you a great starting point for your improvisations. All the notes lie well under the fingers and generally sound good together. **"**

Major pentatonic scales

The major pentatonic scale uses notes 1, 2, 3, 5 and 6 of a major scale and has a very natural feel to it. It's commonly used in jazz and popular music – in fact, there are a huge number of pop songs based entirely on the major pentatonic scale!

Starting to improvise on the black notes

Play a pentatonic scale starting on F♯ – this uses all the black notes and is ideal to improvise with. Notice that the interval from note 3 to 5 is a minor 3rd (one semitone smaller than a major 3rd).

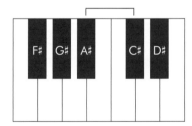

Try improvising over these two backing tracks – any black note will fit. Here's how to get started:
- Play up and down the black-note scale in time with the backing track.
- Then try skipping some notes of the scale.
- Finally try adding different rhythms, using only a few notes of the scale.

㉓ **Black-note boogie**

㉔ **Black magic**

Listening post: Well-known songs that use the pentatonic scale

Auld Lang Syne Trad.
Stairway to Heaven Led Zeppelin
Swing Low, Sweet Chariot Trad.
Old Macdonald Had a Farm Trad.
Just the Two of Us Bill Withers
Summertime George Gershwin
Chameleon Herbie Hancock

Perfect pentatonic practice

Now that you're familiar with how the major pentatonic scale sounds, let's try it in different keys. Have a go at playing these four scales over each backing track rhythm.

- Try hands separately at first, then hands together.
- Try skipping some notes of the scale or mixing up the note order to create your own melodies.
- Try playing the scale / melody using different rhythms.
- Finally, work out how to play a pentatonic scale starting on D and E flat.

Listening post

The power of the pentatonic scale Bobby McFerrin

25 C major pentatonic

26 G major pentatonic

27 F major pentatonic

28 B♭ major pentatonic

Filling in the gaps

Improvise over the left-hand chords, using notes from the pentatonic scale given.
Start off by improvising over the backing track given.

29 **Pentatonic magic 1**

Improvise pentatonic responses in the right and then left hand.

Can you remember the scale each time?

Spice it up!

Gentle waltz

Spinning

Minor pentatonic scales

Here are some minor pentatonic scales. Use them to improvise over the
backing tracks as you did for the major pentatonics.

25 **A minor pentatonic**

26 **E minor pentatonic**

27 **D minor pentatonic**

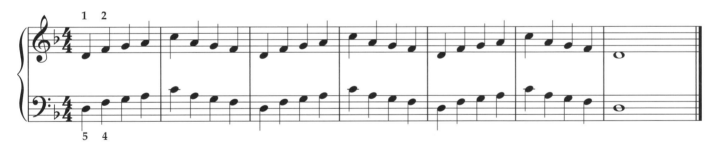

28 **G minor pentatonic**

Improvising with minor pentatonics

Improvise in the boxed bars: try it using the audio tracks first.

31 **Skinny-rib swing**

32 **Summer's end**

33 **Diamond cut**

Session 6
Sing, sing, sing

> **I never sing a song the same way twice.**
> Billie Holiday

Pam says

❝ Good improvisers can always sing what they want to play on the piano – almost as if the piano is an extension of their voice. Do get familiar with your own voice – even if you don't think you can sing! Give it a go. It will really help you to play what you want when you improvise.

So it's time to get those vocal chords going. The following tunes will help build vocal confidence – sing along with each track. **❞**

34 Amazing grace
Amazing grace!
How sweet the sound
That saved a wretch like me.
I once was lost but now am found,
Was blind but now I see.

35 When the saints
Oh when the saints
Go marching in,
Oh when the saints go marching in,
I want to be in that number,
Oh when the saints go marching in.

36 Danny boy
Oh Danny boy, the pipes, the pipes are calling
From glen to glen, and down the mountain side.
The summer's gone, and all the roses falling,
It's you, it's you must go and I must bide.
But come ye back when summer's in the meadow,
Or when the valley's hushed and white with snow,
And I'll be here in sunshine or in shadow,
Oh Danny boy, oh Danny boy, I love you so!

Copy Cat

This is a call-and-response singing exercise. Listen to each track all the way through first, then see if you can copy each phrase by singing the response (without looking at the music!). Then check against the music here.

Scat singing

> **The only thing better than singing – is more singing!**
> Ella Fitzgerald

Scat is often used for vocal improvisations – the singer uses nonsense sounds rather than words. Scat gives singers the ability to improvise melodies and create the sounds of an instrumental solo.

It was American artists like Ella Fitzgerald, Sarah Vaughan and Mel Tormé who took scatting to a high art form in the later years of jazz's development, from the late 1940s to the 1970s. Ella Fitzgerald (1917–1996), often considered the greatest scat singer, was referred to as the Lady of Song, the Queen of Jazz and Lady Ella! She was known for her pure tone, beautiful phrasing and a horn-like improvisational quality in her scat singing. More recently, one artist has taken scatting to new heights. Vocal improviser Bobby McFerrin's performances have shown that 'wordless' singing has travelled a long way from the original concept demonstrated by Louis Armstrong, Gladys Bentley, Cab Calloway, Anita O'Day and Leo Watson.

Pam says

" Scat singing is a fantastic way to free up your voice. Try singing in the bath if you don't want anyone else to listen to your efforts, and remember – anything goes! "

42 Here is a fun exercise that will help you to build confidence and rhythm.
* Listen to **Track 42** and sing back each 2-bar phrase.
* Play the track again and sing the scat words 'doo' or 'bee' (or anything you like) on the responses, making up your own rhythm.
* Next try singing a short improvised phrase, then play it back to yourself on the piano.

Pam says

" Don't worry if you find this tricky – try listening to some great singers instead. That can be just as valuable. "

Listening post: Scat

One Note Samba, Blue Skies Ella Fitzgerald
Heebie Jeebies, Hotter Than That Louis Armstrong
The Scat Song Cab Calloway
Everybody Jam Scatman John

Session 7
Making friends with scales

> Master your instrument, master the music, and then forget all that and just play.
> Charlie Parker

Right-hand finger tricks

When you are improvising you'll find that knowing your scales – and some finger tricks – will come in useful. Learn these from memory.

Scale trick 1

Try playing this pattern in D major as well.

Scale trick 2

Try playing these in F major and D major as well.

Left-hand finger tricks

Scale trick 1

Try playing this pattern starting in D as well.

Scale trick 2

Introducing the natural minor

Every major scale has a **relative minor** – they share the same key
signature. You can find a relative minor by going down 3 semitones from
the major. The **natural minor** is different to the harmonic minor only in that
it has no raised 7th note. This is A natural minor:

Pam says

❝We will only be using the natural minor for improvising –
it's much easier. **❞**

Natural minor finger tricks

A natural minor

E natural minor

Know your arpeggios

Arpeggios are made up of the 1st, 3rd and 5th notes of any scale. Being comfortable playing arpeggio patterns will also really help you when improvising. Here are some patterns to practise and learn – try them in different keys, too.

Arpeggio finger tricks 1

Arpeggio finger tricks 2

Can you play this in F major and A minor?

Memorising your scales and arpeggios will give you lots of confidence and ideas for improvising! Learn this next piece from memory, listening to it first, then repeating each two-bar phrase until you know it.

Pam says

> " Use the pedal every two bars in this study – it'll sound better. "

43 Performance piece **Arpeggio Express**

Jamming in the major and minor groove

It's time to take some more steps into full improvisation. Here's a checklist to get you ready:

- Listen to the backing track and be aware of the key it's in.
- Play the scale of the track with your right hand.
- Play along with the track, using the melodic ideas given. Keeping it very simple, improvise some ideas for the last four bars.
- Try to repeat short phrases and vary the rhythm.
- Remember there are no mistakes when you improvise!

> There are no wrong notes, some are just more right than others.
> Thelonius Monk

44 **C major** (swing style groove)

45 **A minor** (Latin style, straight)

46 **F major** (pop groove)

Session 8
Understanding chords

A chord is simply more than one note played at the same time. A chord symbol indicates a particular set of three (or more) notes.

The symbol for a **major chord** is the capital letter of the name of the major triad (notes 1, 3 and 5 of the scale):

The symbol for a **minor chord** is the capital letter of the minor triad followed by an 'm' (= minor).

Here are the chords (or triads) of some major keys:

Here are the chords (or triads) of some minor keys:

Inversions

Changing the order of the notes in a chord or triad (so a different note is at the bottom rather than the 1st note) makes it easier to move from one chord to another and can sound better. An inversion is indicated in chord symbols by adding a slash after the chord name, followed by the name of the note at the bottom of the chord:

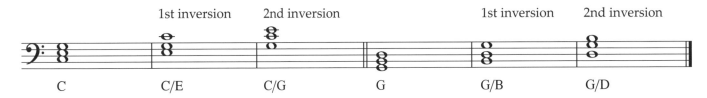

Practise playing these in F and A minor as well.

> **What does music mean to you?**
> **What would you do without music?**
> Duke Ellington

Introduction to leadsheets

A leadsheet shows you just the melody line, lyrics and chords symbols of
a song – so all the information is included on one stave line.

If no chords are to be played it's indicated with 'NC'.

Here's an example:

The Rose

Words and Music
by Amanda McBroom

Pam says

> ❝Many jazz musicians use leadsheets as a starting point, so you'll
> need to know how to use one. Have a go!❞

- First of all, play just the chords in the left hand, in the order they're given.

- Consider which chords were awkward because you had to move a long
  way. Try using inversions so you don't have to move as far. You can mark
  these inversions on the music to help you.

- When you're comfortable with the left-hand chords, trying adding the
  right-hand melody over the top.

Here's another leadsheet. Have a go at playing the chords as indicated along with the melody. Remember to use inversions to make the chord progression smoother.

Swing low sweet chariot

Traditional
arr. Pam Wedgwood

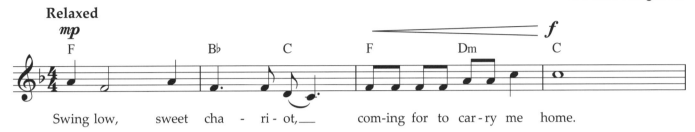

Swing low, sweet cha - ri - ot,— com-ing for to car-ry me home.

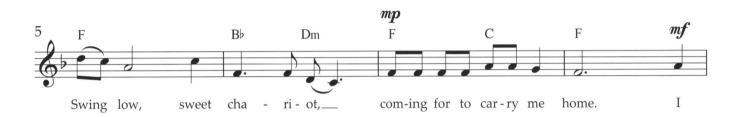

Swing low, sweet cha - ri - ot,— com-ing for to car-ry me home. I

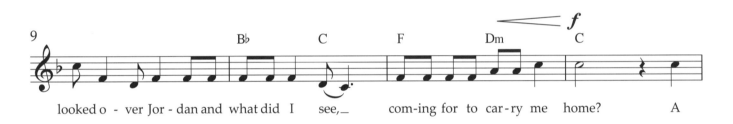

looked o - ver Jor - dan and what did I see,— com-ing for to car-ry me home? A

band— of an - gels com-ing af - ter me,— com-ing for to car-ry me home.

Swing low, sweet cha - ri - ot,— com-ing for to car-ry me home.

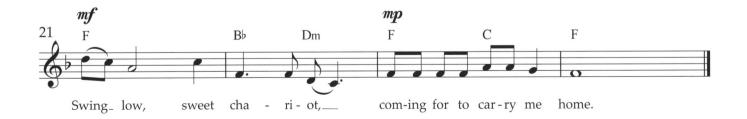

Swing— low, sweet cha - ri - ot,— com-ing for to car-ry me home.

Different accompaniment styles

Splitting the chord: you don't need to play all 3 notes of the triad together:

Inversions of the chords: sound smoother and less heavy:

Two-note chords, using a descending bassline:

Here is another leadsheet to try. This time experiment with different accompaniment styles.

Sunny afternoon

Words and Music
by Ray Davies

Improvising over chords

Try to fit a simple melody over these accompaniments. Use the suggested openings to give you ideas and make up your own titles.

> **Do not fear mistakes – there are none!**
> Miles Davis

47

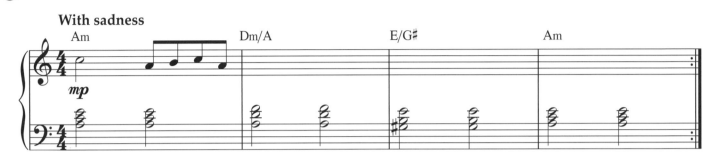

48

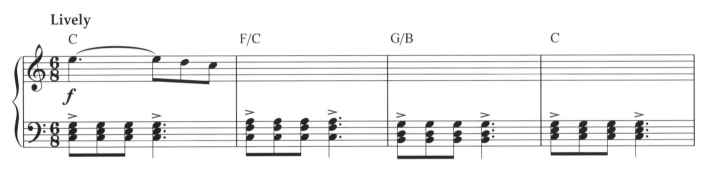

49

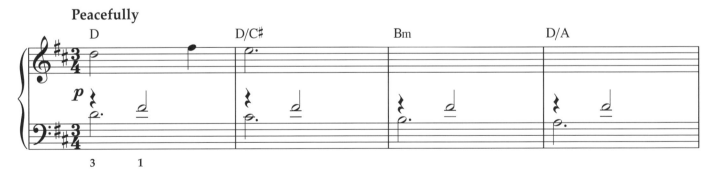

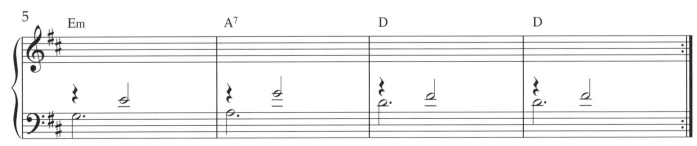

Session 9
Chords with a seventh

Chords can have more than three notes: it's very common in jazz to add a 7th: an interval of a seventh from the root (bottom) note of the chord. Here are the three most useful types of seventh chord.

The dominant seventh

You will come across dominant seventh chords a lot, particularly when playing blues. This chord is built on the fifth note (dominant) of any scale, and it is made up of the 1st, major 3rd, 5th and minor (or flattened) 7th notes. It sounds like it needs to resolve down a fifth to the tonic (the chord on the first note of the scale).

Pam says

❝ Dominant is an important word, so try to remember it! ❞

Dominant seventh chords are indicated by the chord name followed by a 7. Here's a dominant seventh in the key of C, built on the fifth note, G.

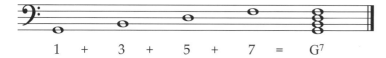

$$1 \quad + \quad 3 \quad + \quad 5 \quad + \quad 7 \quad = \quad G^7$$

If you play it, you will hear that it needs to resolve to the chord of C major:

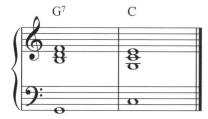

Here are some dominant seventh chords resolving in other keys.
Play them to get used to how they sound.

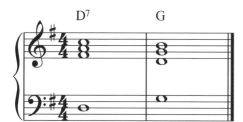
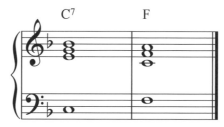
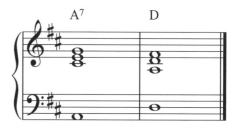

The major seventh

This is another important chord that is used in many different styles of music. A major seventh is built the same way as a dominant seventh, but using the major seventh note of the scale. This chord is indicated by the chord name and maj7 (or M7 or a Δ).

So C major seventh looks like this:

Here are a few examples of major 7th chords. Play these to get used to how they sound – and then try them in different inversions.

The minor seventh

Constructed the same way as the previous seventh chords, this chord uses the notes of the natural minor scale (so no raised seventh). Here are some examples of minor sevenths:

40

Dominant seventh doodle

Can you resolve the following chords? The first is done for you. Try to keep
the bottom note of the chord the same.

50 Circles

In bars 1–6 you can see how the dominant chord resolves to the fifth
below. This is called a circle of fifths. Listen to the chords on the track.

51 Improvising over seventh chords

Use any white notes to improvise a right-hand melody over these left-hand chords.

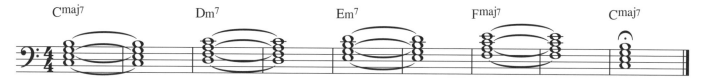

52 Seventh doodles

Still just using the white notes, add the chords suggested to the melody given.
Try it with the backing track, then improvise your own version.

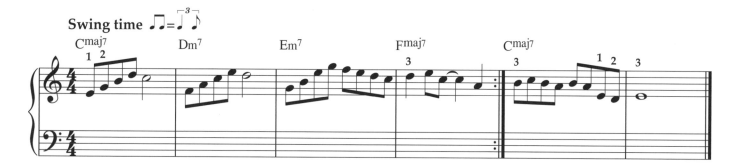

Session 10
Introducing the blues scale

Style spotlight

The blues scale uses the 1st, flattened 3rd, 4th, sharpened 4th, 5th and flattened 7th notes of a major scale:

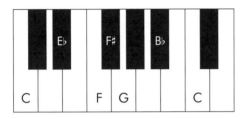

Using this pattern, play the blues scales starting on C, G and F:

Scaletastic!

Try playing these blues scales to the following tracks. The blues scale is used to create a funky/bluesy sound, so do gradually develop the notes and rhythm so you're not just playing the scale up and down.

53 **C blues scale** (swung)

54 **G blues scale** (swung)

55 **F blues scale** (swung)

Pam says

"Listen to as much live music as you can – you will always remember those performances. **"**

> **Of course there are a lot of ways you can treat the blues, but it will still be the blues.**
> Count Basie

Listening post:
different blues styles

The Thrill is Gone BB King
Hoochie Coochie Man
Muddy Waters
Love in Vain Eric Clapton

42

Blues scale on C

Here are some more tracks to improvise over, this time with some starting points:

56 Doodle do-dah

57 Busy bee blues

Listening post

One of my all-time favourites is the recording
of **Slow Blues** by Count Basie and Oscar
Peterson. What a duo!

Swinging the Blues Count Basie

Everyday I Have the Blues Ray Charles

The Way Back Blues Erroll Garner

St Louis Blues Ella Fitzgerald

Blues scale on G

Notebank

58 ## Pot Luck 1

59 ## Pot Luck 2

Blues scale on F

Notebank

Now try improvising 2-bar answering phrases:

60 ## Pot Luck 3

61 ## Pot Luck 4

62 Performance piece **Blues étude**

Learn these useful riffs from the pentatonic and blues scale patterns.
Listen to track 62 first.

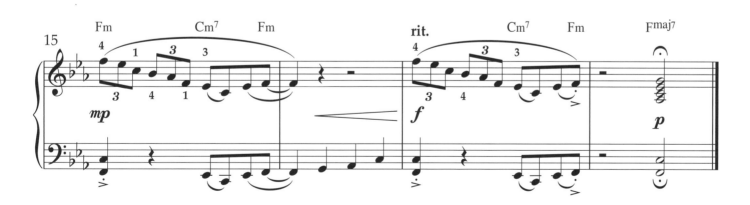

Can you pick out the notes of the G blues scale before you play this?

Look out for seventh notes, too.

Session 11
Understanding musical form

Pam says

❝ It's important to understand how a piece of music is put together to be able to improvise. We need to know what's coming next and how the sections of a piece fit together. ❞

Sections in music are usually represented with a letter – A, B, C, etc. A very common structure is **ternary form**, which is in 3 parts: A B A. In jazz, the A section contains the **head**, which is the whole melody or chorus. The B section is often called the **middle 8**.

A (head)	B (middle 8)	A

- Typically in jazz the head is played to establish the tune, without any improvisation. This also establishes the chords to be used.

- It then moves on to the middle 8 (B section).

- Then a return to the head to finish off the piece. It may reappear slightly differently but should be more or less as it was at the beginning.

- In jazz, many tunes have an AABA structure, with a repeat of the first section.

You will need to:
- Memorise the head
- Memorise the chord sequence
- Memorise the scale patterns you'll be using.

> ### Listening post: tunes using ABA or AABA structure
>
> **Twinkle, Twinkle Little Star**
> **Over the Rainbow**
> **Body and Soul** Carly Simon
> **Have You Met Miss Jones?** Frank Sinatra
> **Lullaby of Birdland** Ella Fitzgerald
> **Satin Doll** Duke Ellington
> **Take Five** Dave Brubeck
> **Softly, as in a Morning Sunrise** Abbey Lincoln
> **Take the A train** Ella Fitzgerald

64 Performance piece **Rock solid**

This piece is based on a simple ABA structure. Play through it using the backing
track and adding in left-hand chords in the same style in the B section.

65 Performance piece **Headstrong**

With the da capo structure this is in AABA form. Fill in the B section left
hand yourself. Remember – you need to memorise the head melody and
chord sequence before you can improvise! Track 65 provides a backing
track to play along with.

Pam says

❝ Try working out the structure of other pieces you have played. **❞**

Session 12
The 12-bar blues

Pam says

❝ When we think of the blues we often think of sad music, but actually the blues is simply a way of telling the world how you feel through music. Perhaps you're feeling sorry for yourself, or are feeling joyful and uplifted – many different emotions can be expressed when playing the blues! The blues evolved in the 19th century when African slaves sang spirituals, chants and work songs whilst working in the fields. ❞

The basic 12-bar blues originally used just three chords:
• The 7th chord built on the 1st note of the scale
• The 7th chord built on the 4th note of the scale
• The 7th chord built on the 5th note of the scale.

Try playing the chords in C major:

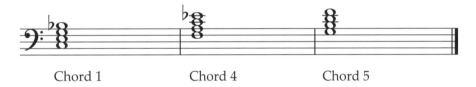

Chord 1   Chord 4   Chord 5

This is the order of those three chords in a typical 12-bar sequence. (There are variations on this sequence!)

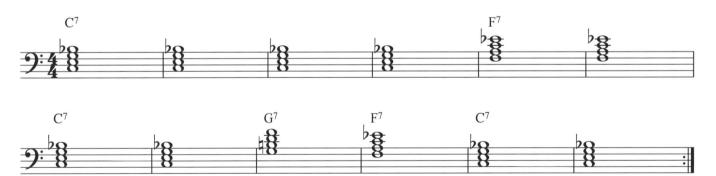

> **Listening post**
>
> These songs all use the 12-bar blues as a basic structure. Notice how the tempo of each song varies – blues doesn't have to be slow! My favourite is **Give Me One Reason** Tracy Chapman.
>
> **I Got You (I Feel Good)** James Brown
>
> **What'd I Say** Ray Charles
>
> **Tutti Frutti** Little Richard
>
> **Before You Accuse Me** Eric Clapton

Starting to improvise the 12-bar blues

For each of these pieces, start by playing the left-hand chords along with the backing track, then try adding in the missing right-hand melody. Keep it very simple – use just a few notes until you are confident. The notes of the blues scale may clash with the chords – but this is what playing the blues is about!

Chord symbols are not repeated if the chord stays the same. The tracks given are backings only for you to improvise over.

66 **Blues for buddy**

Chord 1   Chord 4

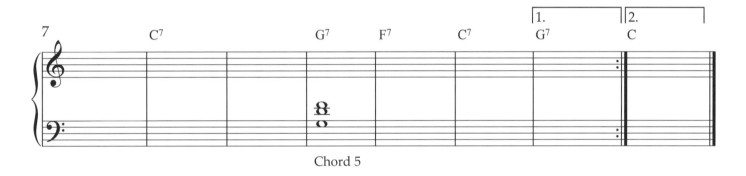

Chord 5

67 **Baker Street blues**

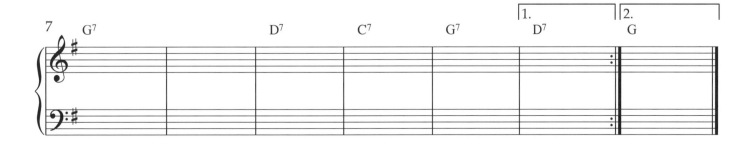

Heads and Tails

Session 13
Getting started with modes

Pam says

❝ Modes are often used in jazz improvisation – they create a different sound and add interest to your melody. **❞**

Style spotlight

Modes are types of scales from ancient Greece. There are seven modes, each based on a different pattern of tones and semitones: Ionian, Dorian, Phrygian, Lydian, Mixolydian, Aeolian and Locrian. You can work out the pattern for each by starting each modal scale on a different degree of a C major scale (using the white notes only). We're going to use just one of them for now – the Dorian mode.

The Dorian scale

This scale runs from D to D. It sounds similar to the natural minor scale. You can start a Dorian scale on other notes, using the same pattern. Here it is starting on D (using the key signature of C major) and C (using the key signature of B flat major):

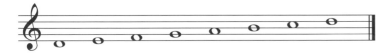

Pam says

❝ I really like the sound of this scale! I think you'll enjoy improvising with these notes … **❞**

Listening post: well-known tunes in the Dorian mode

Scarborough Fair Traditional
Eleanor Rigby The Beatles
Toccata and fugue in D minor JS Bach

Dorian drills

Play straight and swung.

Dorian on D

Dorian on E

Dorian on F

Dorian on G

Using the Dorian mode

When you are improvising it's a great idea to think about all the scales you can use on the journey. Start by choosing keys on the white notes – D Dorian is easiest!

Pam says

❝Try these Dorian doodles and play along with the backing tracks. The first will help you get used to the sound and feel of the Dorian mode. In the second you can begin improvising!❞

69 Dorian doodle 1

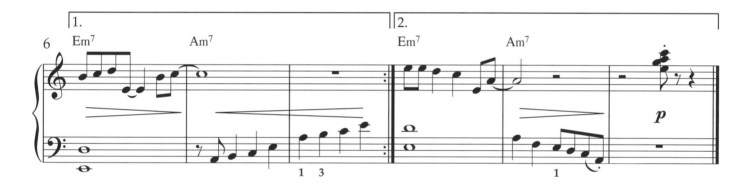

70 Dorian doodle 2

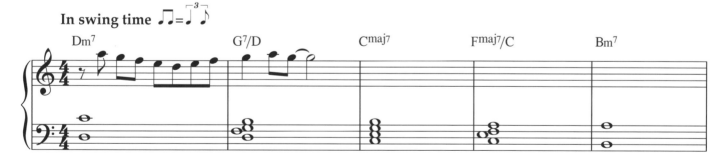

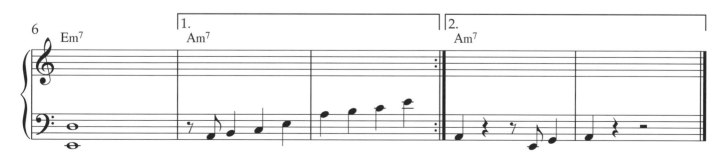

Session 14
Walking bass lines

Style spotlight

A walking bass line is a common accompaniment in jazz styles – it is a bass part that typically moves in a regular ♩ ♩ ♩ movement, giving a walking feel. Before the advent of jazz, the bass line would often play on beats 1 and 3 (in 4 time). In jazz, more movement was needed so the bass line moved on every beat – hence the walking bass!

Create your own walking bass line

1 Work out and play these three chords:
Dm^7 – G^7 – C^{maj7} – C^{maj7}

2 Play the bottom note of each chord in the left hand before adding the right hand. Repeat until you know it well and can play it from memory:

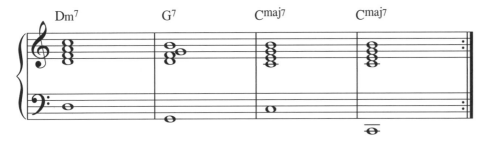

3 Now play the bottom note as ♩ ♩ – change the octave if you like.

4 Try moving to the fifth note above the root each time:

5 Now play that with four beats in a bar:

6 Try adding the middle note of the chord (the 3rd):

7 For the next stage, you can alternate the notes of each chord:

8 Try adding a chromatic passing note on the fourth beat – a semitone up or down to the next chord.

9 Let's try a pattern now – the root, 3rd, 5th then a chromatic note:

Invent your own walking bass using this chord progression. Keep it simple and follow the ideas above to develop it. Write it down if that helps.

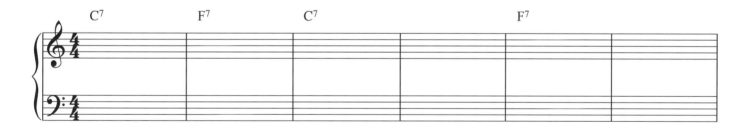

Walking bass-line workouts

71 **F blues**

Here's a walking bass line using an interval-style bass – it sounds quite
groovy! Can you play the chords suggested in the right hand to accompany
the left hand on the backing track?

72 **Easy does it!**

Here's an example of a scale-type bass line.

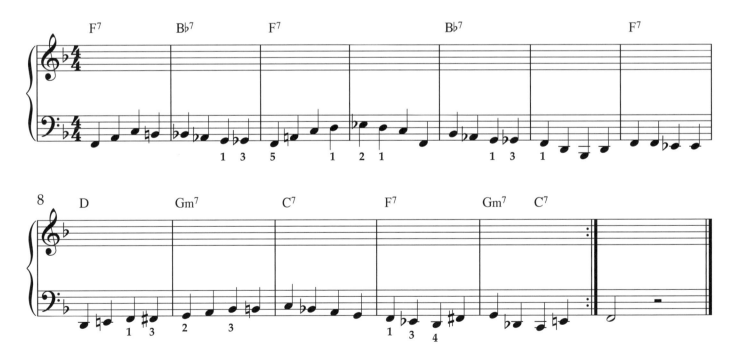

Session 15
A taste of Latin styles

Pam says

> **"** There are many different types of Latin music. These styles have a huge influence in jazz and pop music so you should be familiar with the main three styles. **"**

Style spotlight

Bossa nova loosely means 'new trend' in Portuguese and is a popular form of Brazilian music that developed from Latin samba rhythms and West Coast cool jazz. Although bossa nova became popular in the early 1950s, the word 'bossa' had been used since the 1930s to describe anything current in popular culture. By the 1950s 'bossa' also described a musician with a highly individual style. It usually has quite a relaxed feel, and is not generally swung.

Try the exercise and *Hot 'n' spicy* on page 60 for an example of bossa nova style.

Samba is one of the most popular music and dance styles from Brazil. It developed in Rio de Janeiro in the early 20th century and became the dance most associated with Rio's carnival. With its strong, syncopated rhythm, samba has become known throughout the world.

Play the rhythm and piece *Sizzling samba* on page 61.

Originally the word **rumba** also meant party in Cuba and on Sunday afternoons in Havana it's still not unusual to see Cubans using drums made out of stools, old tables and glass bottles, into spontaneous song and dance. The dance form of the rumba is seductive and slow, and tells a romantic story of two lovers dancing together. This music and dance form emerged in the mid-19th century.

Play *Raspberry rumba* and its exercise on page 62.

Listening post: Latin

Tico Tico Charlie Parker
Samba Sensative/Wave Oscar Peterson
Watermelon Man Mongo Santamaria

The Girl from Ipanema
Desafinado Ella Fitzgerald
Take Five Dave Brubeck

73 Listen to, then try this bossa nova rhythm. Drum the rhythm on a table top before you begin.

74 Performance piece **Hot 'n' spicy**

75 Practise this rhythm pattern for 'Sizzling samba'.

76 Performance piece **Sizzling samba**

With a slow samba beat

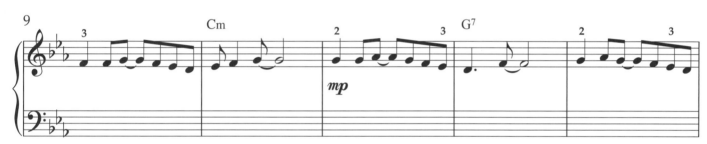

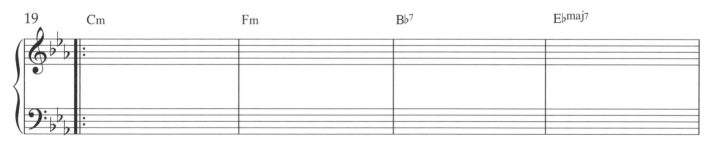

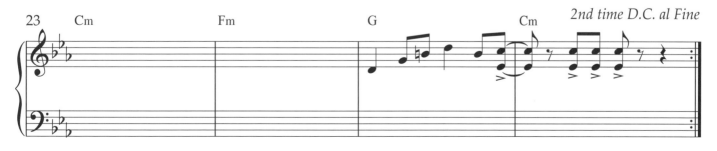

77 Here's a workout to help you get the feel of a typical rumba rhythm.

78 Performance piece **Raspberry rumba**

Glossary of chord symbols

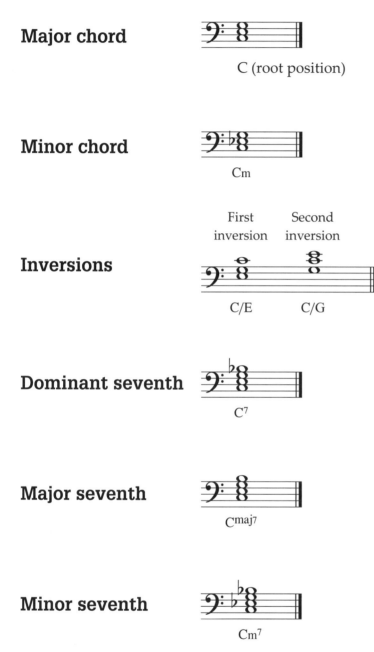

Major chord — C (root position)

Minor chord — Cm

Inversions — First inversion C/E — Second inversion C/G

Dominant seventh — C⁷

Major seventh — Cmaj7

Minor seventh — Cm⁷

Glossary of terms

12-bar blues a progression based on 3 chords (I, IV, V) that is very common in popular music.

Arpeggio the 1st, 3rd and 5th notes of any scale.

Call and response a musical phrase that is answered by a second phrase.

Blues scale the 1st, flattened 3rd, 4th, sharpened 4th, 5th and flattened 7th notes of a scale.

Bossa nova a Latin style that has a relaxed feel and syncopated rhythm.

Chord more than one note played at the same time.

Chord symbol an indication of a particular set of 3 (or more) notes.

Chord inversions changing the order of notes in a chord so a note other than the root is at the bottom.

Chord sequence a particular progression of chords.

Dominant the 5th note of a scale.

Dominant 7th chord a chord made up of the 1st, 3rd, 5th and minor 7th notes that wants to resolve to a chord a 5th below.

Dorian mode a scale running from D to D with no sharps or flats.

Head the opening (A) section of a piece.

Interval the distance between one note and another.

Jazz waltz a jazzy style in 3 time, usually featuring syncopation.

Leadsheet the melody line, lyrics and chord symbols of a song.

Major 7th chord built of the 1st, 3rd, 5th and 7th notes of a major scale.

Major pentatonic scale a scale made up of 5 notes: the 1st, 2nd, 3rd, 5th and 6th notes of a scale.

Middle 8 the middle (B) section of a piece.

Minor 7th chord built of the 1st, 3rd, 5th and 7th notes of a natural minor scale.

Minor pentatonic scale a scale made up of the 1st, 3rd, 4th, 5th and 7th notes of the natural minor scale.

Modes ancient Greek scales in 7 different patterns of tones and semitones.

Natural minor a minor key or scale with no raised 7th.

NC no chord.

Ragtime a style of piano music that features syncopated rhythm in the right-hand with a regular left-hand accompaniment.

Relative minor the minor key with the same key signature as a major key.

Riff a short, repeated phrase.

Root the bottom note of a triad.

Root position a chord with the root (bottom note) at the base of the chord.

Rumba a seductive Latin style with a relatively slow tempo.

Samba a Latin style that features strong syncopated rhythm, energetic tempo and often voluptuous dance moves.

Scat singing singing with nonsense sounds rather than words.

Straight ♩♩ that are not to be swung are called 'straight'.

Swing rhythm ♩♩ that are played slightly unevenly or 'swung'.

Syncopation a rhythm which is played off the main beat(s) of the bar.

Ternary form a piece in 3 sections: A B A.

Tonic the first note (or root) of a chord or scale.

Triad a 3-note chord made up of the 1st, 3rd and 5th notes of a scale.

Walking bass line a bass line that generally moves in a regular ♩ ♩ ♩ ♩ movement, giving a walking feel.